רבנו בחיי

בין אדם לחברו

Between Man
and his
Fellow Man

Translated and Annotated by

Rabbi Dr. Charles B. Chavel

Shilo Publishing House, Inc.
New York, N.Y. 10002

Contents

From Rabbeinu Bachya's KAD HAKEMACH/ENCYCLOPEDIA OF TORAH THOUGHTS, published by Shilo Publishing House Inc.

Some references in the footnotes refer to other chapters of the above work.

Rabbeinu Bachya Ben Asher

Rabbeinu Bachya was born around 1260 in Saragossa, Spain, and died in 1340. He was a disciple of Rabbeinu Shlomo Ben Aderet, the famed Rashba, who was the foremost personality of his generation.

The era in which Rabbeinu Bachya flourished was a stormy one, for the Jewish Community was beset with problems from within and without. The Church was utilizing every means possible—from ordinary missionary work to elaborate public disputations—in order to achieve the conversion of the Jews, or failing that, to make their lives miserable. Within the Jewish Community itself there was a struggle raging between the pro-Maimonists, and the anti-Maimonists. Moreover, the Spanish government fell more and more under the influence of the Church which gradually began to turn the Golden Era of Spanish Jewry into a thing of the past.

In this period of storm and stress, Rabbeinu Bachya first made his voice heard as a preacher in the Synagogues of Saragossa and perhaps those of Barcelona as well.

Preaching was not the only activity of Rabbeinu Bachya, for he was also deeply involved with writing. He wrote four major works, which live on through the generations: His great Commentary on the Torah, which was completed in 1291, The Kad Hakemach, The Shulchon Shel Arba, and a commentary on Tractate Avos.

The Kad Hakemach, written after the completion of the Commentary on the Torah contains sixty discourses on various topics arranged according to the Hebrew alphabet. These discourses were written in pure classical Hebrew and occupy a unique place in Hebrew sacred literature.

Among the sixty themes in the Kad Hakemach we find a golden thesaurus of Jewish thought and ethics. It contains not only discussions for all seasons of the year, but also topics of paramount importance in the life of the individual and of society as a whole. In short, this work is a notable contribution to our understanding of those basic Torah concepts which form the core of Jewish life.

גאוה

Haughtiness

The two types of pride—a high opinion of one's achievement and a sense of satisfaction stemming from one's evil ways—are both despicable / Statements of the Sages on haughtiness of the spirit / An overbearing spirit is recognizable in one's conduct, speech and deed, and all the more in his performance of the Divine Commandments / The Torah has prohibited both the High Priest and the king from indulging in pride or haughtiness / To avoid the pitfalls of the sin of haughtiness, it is not enough to assume the moderate course of mere humility. One must rather tend towards the opposite extreme, which is meekness / The meaning of meekness / The reward of those who are meek in spirit.

Haughtiness

THE FEAR OF THE ETERNAL IS TO HATE EVIL, PRIDE,
AND ARROGANCE; AND THE EVIL WAY, AND PERVERSE
SPEECH DO I HATE.[1]

Solomon related this verse in the name of Wisdom, which dictates
that one who fears G-d will despise an evil person,[2] just as [the verse]
and I am prayer[3] means "*and I am* a man of *prayer.*" An evil person is
one of *pride, and arrogance, and the evil way, and perverse speech.*[1]
Solomon mentioned pride first because it is the most objectionable of
all human characteristics. Whoever possesses it is called *an abomination to the Eternal.*[4]

There are two types of pride. A person may pride himself over his
wisdom, his dignified way of life, the good attributes of his character,
and his being more fortunate than the rest of his generation, and a person may pride himself over his evil qualities and all his deeds of *oppres-
sion and perverseness.*[5] Of course, the Sages detest one who takes
satisfaction in deeds incited by the evil inclination, but the Sages also
abhor one who entertains a high opinion of his merit because of his
good deeds, as they said in the Midrash,[6] "Israel is likened to a vine, to

---

(1) Proverbs 8:13. The sense of the verse is simply that it is not enough to avoid doing evil, but to have an abhorrence thereof, and of all that can be classified as
evil. (2) Thus, the expression *to hate evil* means "*to hate* a person, who is *evil.*" — The
collective body of Wisdom, personified in Scripture, is here speaking to Solomon dic-
tating to him rightful principles of life. (3) Psalms 109:4. (4) Proverbs 16:5: *Every
one that is proud in heart is an abomination to the Eternal.* (5) Isaiah
30:12. (6) Midrash Shmuel, 16.

2

teach us that just as a vine has large and small clusters of grapes, the larger ones hanging lower than the smaller ones, so is Israel," [the greater the person the profounder his meekness].

Solomon mentioned *perverse speech*[1] because pride, which is one of the aspects of the evil way of life, causes a person to speak perversely. Pride forces him to deviate from the way of truth and to speak of things which are unfounded.

Our Sages commented,[7] "Whoever is haughty should be chopped down like an *asheirah* (a tree devoted to idolatry),[8] for here it is written, *and the high ones of stature shall be hewn down,*[9] and there it is said, *and hew down their asheirim.*"[10] The Sages further stated,[7] "The Divine Presence cries over one who is haughty, as it is said, *and the haughty He knoweth from afar.*"[11]

The severity of the prohibition against pride applies to a person's activities in the areas of his speech and the practical affairs between him and his fellow man. His arrogance is discernible if he speaks haughtily, as it is written, *He that exalteth his gate seeketh destruction.*[12] The term *gate* is a metaphor for the mouth, for the mouth is to the body as a gate is to a house. His arrogance is recognized in his deeds if he deals with things that are too great and too wonderful for him, as David said, *Neither did I exercise myself in things too great or too wonderful for me.*[13] Needless to say, it is a sin of great magnitude and of harsh punishment to pride oneself in the performance of the commandments [in matters] between himself and the Creator, and to entertain a high opinion of one's own importance while

---

(7) Sotah 5a.   (8) The thought conveyed by the Sages is that even as we are charged to remove idolatry by utterly uprooting it, so should a person who wishes to rid himself of his presumptuousness be prepared to uproot this evil trait in all its manifestations, for impertinence is a form of self-worship (Maharsha, *ibid.*).   (9) Isaiah 10:33.   (10) Deuteronomy 7:5.   (11) Psalms 138:6. G-d brings the humble near Himself, but not the arrogant. He knows the latter from afar and mourns over them (Maharsha, Sotah 5a).   (12) Proverbs 17:19.   (13) Psalms 131:1.

disrespecting the commandment, as in the case of one who exalts himself when walking to the synagogue while carrying the palm branch, and other similar instances.

The Sages said,[14] "One who parades in a scholar's cloak to which he is not entitled is denied entry into the Divine Presence, for here it is written, *The haughty man abideth not,*[15] and there it is written, *to Thy holy abiding place.*"[16] In Tractate Sanhedrin, we find [the following]:[17] "Jeroboam's haughtiness drove him out of the World [to Come], for it is said, *And Jeroboam said in his heart: 'Now will the kingdom return to the House of David.*[18] *If this people go up to bring offerings in the House of the Eternal at Jerusalem, then will the heart of this people turn back unto their lord, even unto Rehoboam, King of Judah.*[19] By tradition, only the kings of the House of David may sit in the Sanctuary Court. When the people will see Rehoboam sitting and me standing, they will say that Rehoboam is the king, and Jeroboam is his servant. If I sit down, however, they will say that I am rebelling against the Kingdom [of David] and they will kill me.' Thereupon, *The king took counsel, and made two calves of gold, and he said unto them: Ye have gone up long enough to Jerusalem; behold thy gods, O Israel,* etc."[20] [In Tractate Sanhedrin], it is further written:[17] "G-d said to

---

(14) Baba Bathra 98a.   (15) Habakkuk 2:5.   (16) Exodus 15:13. The aforementioned verse, *The haughty man 'abideth' not* is thus explained by the present verse, that he is not privileged to be in His *holy abiding place.* — The reason for the punishment is generally explained as follows: Since he parades in a scholar's cloak to which he is not entitled, he is of course a person who speaks falsehoods, of whom it has been said, *he that speaketh falsehood shall not be established before Mine eyes* (Psalms 101:7.)   (17) Sanhedrin 101b.   (18) I Kings 12:26.   (19) *Ibid.,* Verse 27. This occurred just after Jeroboam had established the Kingdom of Israel by leading ten tribes away from the Kingdom of Judah. Jeroboam feared that if his subjects would make the festival pilgrimage to Jerusalem, Rehoboam, King of Judah would regain their loyalty for the reason explained further in the text. To keep his people away from Jerusalem, Jeroboam introduced idolatry into his realms.   (20) *Ibid.,* Verse 28.

Jeroboam, 'Repent, and I and you and [David] the son of Jesse will walk about in the Garden of Eden.' Jeroboam answered, 'Who will be at the head?' G-d replied, '[David] the son of Jesse will be at the head.' Thereupon, Jeroboam said, 'If so, I do not want it.' "[21]

One who is proud by nature usurps "the garb of the King," as it is said, *The Eternal reigneth, He is clothed in majesty,*[22] for majesty befits G-d alone and not any mortal being. He alone is exalted over all existence, and this is also so in this lower world where He subdues the sinners and rebels, who would otherwise have brought about the destruction and foundering of the world as a punishment for their arrogance. Thus, the verse continues, *Yea, the world is established, that it cannot be moved.*[22] Scripture teaches you thereby that were it not that He is exalted over the presumptuous and brings them low unto the earth and subdues them, the world would have foundered.

Our Sages commented:[23] "One who is haughty denies the essence of religion, as it is said, *Then thy heart be lifted up, and thou forget the Eternal thy G-d.*[24] One who is haughty is considered as if he worshipped idols, for here it is written, *Every one that is proud in heart is an abomination to the Eternal,*[25] and in the case of idolatry it is written, *And thou shalt not bring an abomination into thy house.*[26] The

---

(21) Thus, Jeroboam's haughtiness was his undoing in both worlds. Had he submitted in this one matter and agreed that the king of the House of David should take precedence over himself, he would have gained for himself and his descendants a place of honor in the annals of our people. As it is, however, he is known as "a sinner who caused many to sin" (Aboth 5:20). — It should be noted that the Talmudic text does not mention "David" but merely speaks of *ben Yishai*, literally: "the son of Jesse," who is David. But it may well be translated as "a descendant of Jesse," meaning any king of the House of David. Jeroboam was thus voicing his refusal to be second to Rehoboam. (22) Psalms 93:1. (23) Sotah 4 b. (24) Deuteronomy 8:14. The Torah "deems it unto you as if you had forgotten G-d" (Rashi, Sotah 4 b). (25) Proverbs 16:5. (26) Deuteronomy 7:26. The term *abomination* with which Scripture refers to the haughty man is thus here explained to be a reference to idolatry.

haughty person is also considered to have engaged in the practice of immorality, for there too it is written, *for all these abominations have the men of the land done.*'²⁷ The Sages further declared²³ that one who is haughty will not be resurrected.

The Torah has prohibited even the High Priest from being proud of his high position in the priesthood. Thus, it commanded that he himself take up the ashes from the altar.²⁸ Because he was the person designated to perform the Service in the Sanctuary, he was therefore charged to do this lightly regarded act while he was dressed in the four priestly garments.²⁹ All this served to remind him to shun haughtiness, and to be low and submissive instead.

The Torah also warned the monarch against the evil of haughtiness. Thus, it is written, *that his heart be not lifted up above his brethren, and that he turn not aside from the commandment to the right, or to the left.*³⁰ The Torah thereby admonished the king against being proud of his realm and the breadth of his dominion. Instead, he should regard himself merely as one of *his brethren* who do not possess such power and authority. Although it is natural for a king to indulge in pride over the standing of his kingdom, the Torah [specifically] cautioned him against being proud. How much more does [this warning] apply to all [common] people, [who do not have any reason for pride and arrogance, as does a king]! Even the Holy One, blessed be He, Whom majesty is befitting and Who is clothed therein,²² conducts Himself with humility in His relation with His creatures. This is the meaning of the statement, *The Almighty, Whom we cannot find out,*

---

(27) Leviticus 18:27. The chapter there lists all kinds of illicit intercourse. (28) *Ibid.*, 6:3. On the Day of Atonement the removal of the ashes was done by the High Priest. On any other day of the year it could be done by any common priest. (29) The four garments of the ordinary priest were the tunic, drawers, turban and belt. In addition to these, the High Priest wore the breastplate, the robe, the upper garment, and the frontlet. The reference here to the "four priestly garments" must necessarily apply to a common priest. (30) Deuteronomy 17:20.

is surpassing in strength.[31] That is to say, we have not found that the Almighty, Who is surpassing in strength, should come to us in a forceful and overbearing manner; [He comes] only with humility and integrity. This is why Scripture mentions the Divine Name *Sha-dai* (Almighty) here because it indicates His wondrous power over the higher forces when He makes the stellar constellations submissive to His will. However, the Divine Name *Sha-dai* is not found with regard to the lower creatures [for their strength is insignificant altogether].

It is known that haughtiness is one extreme of human characteristics while meekness is the opposite extreme. The moderate course between these two traits is humility. In all [other] moral problems, it is always proper to choose the course of moderation, and that is the intent of Solomon's words, *Weigh the path of thy feet.*[32] Just as a balance brings two opposing weights into equilibrium, so should you balance your path between the two extremes [of a particular moral issue]. However, with regard to the evil of haughtiness, it is insufficient to merely remove oneself to the moderate position of humility. Rather, we are charged to attain meekness, the antithesis [of haughtiness]. With respect to this principle, the Sages said,[33] "*M'od m'od* (be exceedingly) low in spirit." They used the double expression *m'od m'od* to teach us that in this case, one should bend towards meekness, the opposite extreme. It is written of Moses our teacher, *And the man Moses was very meek.*[34] The word *very* indicates that Moses was not satisfied with just being humble, which is the moderate course, but he was inclined to meekness.

To be meek does not mean that one should disgrace himself in any matter or allow himself to be tread upon by others, for man, who was created *in the image of G-d,*[35] is precious and therefore must care for

---

(31) Job 37:23.   (32) Proverbs 4:26.   (33) Aboth 4:4.   (34) Numbers 12:3.   (35) Genesis 1:27.

his honor and the high stature of his rational soul. Certainly, if he is a scholar, he should protect the honor of his Torah knowledge. To be meek means, instead, that one should be gentle in word and deed to all people, needless to mention his peers and superiors. He should hear himself reviled and remain silent, and he should forbear relating against one who unwittingly sinned against him on some single occasion.

To show that meekness is as beloved by G-d as haughtiness is despised by Him, He chose to give the Torah on Mount Sinai, as it is written, *the mountain which G-d had desired for His abode.*[36] The Sanctuary in Jerusalem, too, which stood in the land of Benjamin, was not located directly on the top of the mountain, all as a means of indicating meekness and humility. Similarly, the phylactery of the head is not placed on the highest point of the head, but a bit lower, "the place on the head where the child's brain pulsates."[37]

Therefore, one should be careful in these two matters: he should shun haughtiness and adopt meekness. Since one is beloved and the other hated by G-d, a person should emulate Him [in this regard]. Whoever is meek in spirit merits honor and the Divine Glory rests upon him. He merits honor, for Solomon said, *And he that is of a low spirit shall attain to honor.*[38] The Divine Glory rests upon him, as it is said, *For thus said the High and Lofty One, that abideth eternity, Whose Name is Holy, I dwell in the high and holy place, with him also that is of a contrite and humble spirit, to revive the spirit of the humble, and to revive the heart of the contrite ones.*[39]

---

(36) Psalms 68:17. This psalm is devoted to the theme of the Revelation at Sinai. G-d chose to give the Torah on this low mountain rather than on some higher one to indicate that meekness is preferable to haughtiness. (37) Menachoth 37 a. (38) Proverbs 29:23. (39) Isaiah 57:15.

עֲנָוָה
Humility

The praiseworthiness of humility and the qualities connected with it / Scriptural proof that even G-d possesses this quality / One who practices humility is assured of life in the World to Come / The three characteristics that distinguish the disciples of our patriarch Abraham from the disciples of the wicked Balaam / Humility and timidity over committing a sin are signs of the seed of Abraham / The fear of G-d, which entails fear in the heart and 'fear upon the face,' constitutes a fundamental principle of the Torah.

Humility

THE REWARD OF HUMILITY IS THE FEAR OF THE ETER-
NAL, EVEN RICHES, AND HONOR, AND LIFE.[1]

This verse informs us of the praiseworthiness of the trait of humility, for there are many good qualities connected with it. The literal meaning of the verse is that a person derives a fourfold benefit in this world from humility: fear of the Eternal, wealth, honor, and life.

It is known that from a social standpoint, humility has practical connotations. Thus, one should be bashful and patient, and he should honor others and speak of their good qualities. He should listen to his own humiliation and remain quiet. From this practical aspect of humility, a person will advance to the fear of G-d, which is a rational trait. He will also attain wealth, for one who is humble rejoices over his lot. Arrogance diminishes his satisfaction with his wealth, [for an arrogant person is never satisfied with what he has]. On the other hand, one who is humble is satisfied with little, and is indeed wealthy, as the Sages commented,[2] "Who is rich? It is the one who rejoices over his lot." A humble person likewise will derive honor, for when one avoids the pursuit of pleasures, he is satisfied with his status. This itself is a

(1) Proverbs 22:4. Humility is thus the key to the rich rewards of life both spiritually and materially. Spiritually it leads to the attainment of the fear of G-d and avoidance of sin. Materially it brings riches, honor, and long life, as will be explained. (2) Aboth 4:1. In every human desire there is a limit to one's satisfaction, except in the quest for amassing wealth which is unquenchable. There is, therefore, no rich man in the absolute sense, since he always desires to have more. The only truly rich man is "the one who rejoices over his lot." (Midrash Shmuel).

source of honor to him, as it is written, *And he that is of a lowly spirit shall attain to honor,*[3] and it is further stated, *Before honor goeth humility.*[4] Humility will also bring him life. One who pursues after excesses lives a life of distress, for he cannot always attain his desire. His constant worry shortens his life as he concerns himself with a material world which is not his. However, one who rejoices over his lot will not fret over what he did not acquire, and he will thus live a life of peace. In the Midrash, the Sages said:[5] " *'Eikev' (The heel) of humility is the fear of the Eternal.*[1] What wisdom has made as a crown for its head—as it is said, *The head of wisdom is the fear of the Eternal*[6] — humility has made as a sole for its shoe." From this we may learn that the trait of humility is greater than that of wisdom, for the fear of the Eternal, which is at the head of wisdom, is only the sole of humility.

It is known, that every human characteristic has two extremes in addition to its point of moderation. Humility is the intermediate quality between arrogance on one hand and self-effacement on the other. Generally, the moderate course is the correct one which a person should choose for himself, as Solomon said, *Weigh the path of thy feet.*[7] The intent of this advice is that one should proceed between the two extremes just as the indicator of a balance stands precisely between the two plates. [If one so chooses the course of moderation], all his traits will be proper. Thus, Solomon subsequently added, *Turn not to the right hand nor to the left*[8] that is, proceed upon an intermediate course. However, regarding the trait of humility, we are instructed to bend towards the extreme trait of self-effacement, as the Sages said in their ethical instructions in Tractate Aboth:[9] "Be *m'od m'od* (ex-

---

(3) Proverbs 29:23. (4) *Ibid.*, 18:12. (5) Shir Hashirim Rabbah 1:9. (6) Psalms 111:10. (7) Proverbs 4:26. (8) *Ibid.*, Verse 27. See above, *Ga'avah* (Haughtiness), p. 135 where the author discusses the same topic. (9) Aboth 4:4. The concluding phrase, "since the hope of man etc." suggests the following thought. One should never lose himself to desist from his sense of humility even in the face of derision or insult, for one should give thought to the fact that the final end of those who attack him are but dust and worms, and therefore their attacks are insignificant. Why then should he forego his steady composure and humility? (Midrash Shmuel).

ceedingly) lowly of spirit, since the hope of man is the worm." They doubled the word *m'od* to teach people that one should bend towards the extreme trait of self-effacement.

Because humility is so praiseworthy and has mighty consequences which are visible to all, David said that he himself has *a broken and contrite heart*.[10] Although he was a great king, a prophet, and the leader of the seventy elders of the Sanhedrin, he nevertheless went as far as to describe himself as having *a broken and contrite heart*.[10] Similarly, we find that Moses our teacher, the foremost among all the prophets, was praised by Scripture only for his trait of humility rather than any of his other superior qualities, as it says, *Now the man Moses was very meek*.[11] Scripture used the word *very* in order to indicate that Moses did not desire to remain in the intermediate position of being merely humble; he bent away from the moderate course and leaned towards self-effacement. Therefore, Scripture mentioned that he was *very meek*.

In Bereshith Rabbah, the Sages said:[12] "Rabbi Shimon ben Nezira said, 'Who is as humble as G-d? A disciple says to his teacher, Teach me one chapter, and the teacher answers, Go and wait for me in that place. However, it is different with G-d. He said to Ezekiel, *Arise, go forth into the plain, and I will there speak with thee*.[13] When Ezekiel went forth, he found that G-d had preceded him, as it is said, *Then I arose, and went forth into the plain, and, behold, the Glory of the Eternal stood there*.[14] I must conclude, as the psalmist said, that *'Thy condescension hath made me great.'*[15] Rabbi Abba bar Kahana said, 'See G-d's humility! It is said, *And the Eternal said unto me* [Ezekiel]: *This gate shall be shut, it shall not be opened, neither shall any man enter in by it, for the Eternal, the G-d of Israel, hath entered in by it; therefore it shall be shut*.[16] For the sake of his honor, a mortal king

(10) Psalms 51:19. (11) Numbers 12:13. (12) I have been unable to locate this quotation in Bereshith Rabbah, but it is found in Tanchuma, *Ki Thisa* 15, with some variations. (13) Ezekiel 3:22. (14) *Ibid.*, Verse 23. (15) Psalms 18:36. (16) Ezekiel 44:2. The verse is interpreted by the Sages as follows. The "Great Gate" of the Sanctuary proper was not opened by the priests from the outside to enter

must enter through a great gate and not through a small one, but G-d's Glory came in through the small gate.[16] I must conclude, [as the psalmist has said], *Thy condescension hath made me great.*'[15] Rabbi Simon said, 'See G-d's humility! A mortal king first mentions his name and then cites his praiseworthy accomplishments, but G-d first mentions His deeds — as it said, *Bereshith bara* (literally: *In the beginning He created*)[17] — and only afterward does He mention the Name *Elokim (G-d)*' "[17] Thus far the Midrash.[12]

In order to show the extreme importance of humiity and its far-reaching ramifications, the Sages said that one who practices this trait is assured of life in the World to Come. They stated in Tractate Sanhedrin:[18] "They sent the following text from the Land of Israel [to the Sages of Babylon]: 'Who has a share in the World to Come? It is the one who is humble, polite, and meek of spirit, who bends his head when entering and leaving a house, who constantly toils in the study of Torah, and who does not ascribe credit to himself.' The Rabbis ascribed all these qualities to Rav Ulla bar Ahavah." They first mentioned the supreme trait of humility and then noted its practical and spiritual applications. By "polite," they meant that one should gently conduct his affairs with other people. This is the practical aspect of humility. By "meek of spirit," they meant that one should be humble rather than arrogant. This is the spiritual aspect.

In Tractate Aboth, the Sages said:[19] "Whoever has the following three attributes is a disciple of our patriarch Abraham, and whoever

the inside, but instead was opened from the inside into the outside. This was accomplished through two wickets, one to the north and another to the south which were located in the Entrance Hall leading to the Sanctuary. The verse then tells us that the priest entered by the northern door leading into a cell and from the cell into the Sanctuary until he reached the Great Gate and opened it. He was not to use the southern wicket, *for the Eternal, the G-d of Israel hath entered in it.* (Tamid 3:7). This, then, is the meaning of "the small gate" mentioned in the text . (17) Genesis 1:1. The English translation — *In the beginning G-d created . . .* — does not convey this thought properly, due to the nature of English syntax. (18) Sanhedrin 88 b. See above, *Eivel* (Mourning), Part One, at Note 28, where this text is also quoted. (19) Aboth 5:23.

has the following three faults is a disciple of wicked Balaam. The signs of the disciples of our patriarch Abraham are a 'good eye,' [which will be explained below], a humble soul, and a low spirit. However, the signs of the disciples of wicked Balaam are [an evil eye, a haughty soul, and a proud spirit]. What is the distinction between the disciples of our patriarch Abraham and those of wicked Balaam?[20] The disciples of wicked Balaam inherit Gehenna, as it is said, *And Thou, O G-d, wilt bring them down into the pit of destruction,* etc.[21] However, the disciples of our patriarch Abraham enjoy this world and inherit the World to Come, as it is said, *That I may cause those that love Me to inherit substance,* etc."[22]

The explanation of this is as follows: A "good eye" means that one is not jealous of his friend and is as considerate of his friend's honor as he is of his own. A "humble soul" is one who lowers himself before all and who is sympathetic towards people. A "low spirit" refers to the attribute of humility.

Maimonides explained the Mishnah as follows:[23] "A 'good eye' means that a person should be satisfied with what he has, and not pursue excesses. A 'humble soul' refers to restraint, and a 'low spirit' means the extra degree of humility [beyond the course of moderation]. The three faults corresponding to these attributes all involve the obsession for acquiring money. Thus, an 'evil eye' is the opposite of a 'good eye,' a 'haughty soul' is an insatiable desire for pleasures, and a 'proud spirit'

(20) It has been asked: Why does the question of the Mishnah address itself to the distinction between the disciples of Abraham and Balaam, rather than to the differences between the men themselves? The answer, which is of great significance, is that a new movement cannot be judged by its founders, for the good and bad consequences of their theories cannot be ascertained so soon. The truth emerges with time in the behavior of their disciples. In the case of Abraham and Balaam their differences were not immediately perceptible, for Balaam himself spoke very convincingly. However, you can recognize the difference between light and darkness, between our patriarch Abraham and the wicked Balaam, by analyzing the differences between their disciples. (21) Psalms 55:24. (22) Proverbs 8:21. (23) Maimonides' commentary on Aboth 5:23.

is arrogance. The three desirable characteristics described above were publicized as having been the qualities of our patriarch Abraham. Therefore, anyone who lacks these traits is the disciple of wicked Balaam, since such a person obviously adopted Balaam's faults. The trait of restraint in Abraham is evidenced by his statement to Sarah, *Behold now, I know that thou art a fair woman to look upon,*[24] upon which the Sages commented,[25] 'He had never looked at her until now.' This is perfection in restraint. The trait of satisfaction was manifested when Abraham abandoned all the wealth of Sodom and refused to have any benefit from it, as he said, *That I will not take a thread nor a shoe-latchet.*[26] His humility is apparent in his statement, *I am but dust and ashes.*[27] Balaam, on the other hand, was known for his obsession for acquiring money, as it is said, *Because they hired against thee Balaam the son of Beor.*[28] He was a man who pursued pleasures, as evidenced by his counsel to Balak to have the Moabite women entice the Israelites into lewdness. Undoubtedly, a man's advice follows his nature. Balaam's arrogance is expressed in his self-praising statement, *The saying of him who heareth the words of G-d.*"[29]

In Tractate Aboth, the Sages said,[30] "The insolent are destined for Gehenna, and the shamefaced for the Garden of Eden." It is known that humility and shamefacedness in a person indicate that he is of the seed of Abraham, for the nature of children follows that of their father. Thus, Scripture states, *For I have known him* [Abraham], *to the end that he may command his children and his household after him.*[31]

The attribute of humility is one of the ways of G-d, as mentioned above, and we who have received the Torah are commanded to walk in

---

(24) Genesis 12:11. (25) Baba Bathra 16 a. Now, however, approaching Egypt, a land of dark-skinned people, Abraham tells Sarah, he must be concerned about her beauty, since it is now a source of danger to her. (26) Genesis 14:23. (27) *Ibid.*, 18:27. (28) Deuteronomy 23:5. (29) Numbers 24:4. Thus far is the language of Maimonides in his commentary on Aboth 5:23. (30) Aboth 5:25. (31) Genesis 18:19.

His ways, as it is said, *And thou shalt walk in His ways.*[32] Our patriarch Abraham held fast to this trait. Until his descendants, the people of Israel, acquired it, the Torah was not given to them, as it is written of the Revelation[33] at Sinai, *For G-d is come to prove you, and that His fear may be upon your faces, that ye sin not.*[34] Scripture should have said "that His fear may be in your hearts" [rather than *upon your faces*]. However, the Sages commented,[35] "The verse, *His fear upon your faces,* refers to the shamefacedness to sin." The fear of G-d, which entails both the fear in the heart and the "fear upon the face," constitutes the essential principle of the entire Torah, as Solomon stated, *The end of the matter, all having been heard: fear G-d, and keep His commandments, for this is the whole* [duty of] *man.*[36]

(32) Deuteronomy 28:9.   (33) See above, *Aravah,* Note 9.   (34) Exodus 20:17.   (35) Mechilta, *ibid.*   (36) Ecclesiastes 12:13.

שלום
Peace

Peace is the foundation and principle of the entire Torah / Peace is the essential element in the creation and preservation of the world / The greatness of the power of peace / Peace within a city and the management thereof is dependent upon its leaders / The importance of greeting a fellow man / The significance of avoiding dissension and the enemies of peace / The return of the exiles to Jerusalem will be through the merit of peace.

Peace

HER WAYS [THE WAYS OF TORAH] ARE WAYS OF
PLEASANTNESS, AND ALL HER PATHS ARE PEACE.[1]

This verse teaches us that peace is the foundation and principle of
the entire Torah and the essential element in the creation of the world.
Thus, the Sages commented,[2] "At the time of Creation all beings came
into existence with their acquiescence and with pleasure in their form,
for it says, and all 'tz'va'am' (the host of them)."[3]

It is known that the heavens were created first. [The Hebrew term
for heavens is] shamayim, for the heavens are composed of eish (fire)
and mayim (water). These two opposites are held together only
through peace. It is thus written, He maketh peace in His high places.[4]
The expression in His high places denotes two things. First, it refers to
the very heavens, which consist of essential substances [fire and water]
that could not continue to exist together without making peace among
themselves. Second, it refers to G-d's angels in the high places, for He

---

(1) Proverbs 3:17. The Torah does not impose upon man any burdensome tasks,
such as endangering his life or health. On the contrary, all commands of the Torah
contribute to the complete wholesome pleasantness of life, and all its paths are design-
ed to bring peace between man and G-d, and between man and man.   (2) Chullin
60 a.   (3) Genesis 2:10. The Sages in Tractate Chullin 60 a, expounded, "Read not
the word as tz'va'am (their host), but as tzivyonam (their pleasure)," which Rashi,
ibid., interprets, all beings came into existence "according to the shape of their own
choice." Thus, peace and harmony reigned at the Creation.   (4) Job 25:2.

18

makes peace among them, as the Sages commented,[5] *"Dominion and fear are with Him; He maketh peace in His high places.*[4] *Dominion* is a reference to the angel Michael; *and fear* is a reference to the angel Gabriel." Michael consists of water, Gabriel consists of fire, and G-d makes peace between them. In Midrash Shir Hashirim Rabbah, we find:[6] "Rabbi Abin said, 'Not only does G-d make peace between one angel and another, but He does so even within one angel, half of whom is snow and half fire.' Rabbi Yochanan said, *'He maketh peace in His high places.*[4] The heavens are made of water and the stars of fire, yet they do not damage each other. The sun never faces the concave of the moon's crescent.' "[7]

Consider the greatness of the power of peace! Even if Israel would worship idols, the attribute of justice would not be brought to bear against them [immediately] if they were united, as it is said, *Ephraim is joined to idols; let him alone.*[8] The power of peace is great indeed, for the Priestly Blessing concludes with peace, as it is said, . . . *and give thee peace.*[9] Great is the power of peace, for the sake of which the Torah contains accounts such as [Joseph being told by his brothers], *Thy father did command before he died, saying: So shall ye say unto Joseph: Forgive, I pray thee now, the transgression of thy brethren,* etc.[10] Actually, Jacob had never issued such a command; the brothers said it on their own volition.[11]

G-d Himself is called *Shalom* (Peace), as it is said, *And he* [Gideon] *called it* [the altar], *The Eternal is Peace.*[12] It is further written, *The*

(5) Bereshith 12:7.   (6) Shir Hashirim 3:20.   (7) The concave side of the crescent is always away from the sun so that the moon should not feel humiliated by the sun whose light is whole while hers is incomplete. In this way, G-d keeps peace between the sun and moon (Rosh Hashanah 23 b).   (8) Hosea 4:17. Ephraim is a surname for the Kingdom of Israel, consisting of ten tribes, and founded by Jeroboam who was of the tribe of Ephraim.   (9) Numbers 6:26.   (10) Genesis 50:16-17.   (11) Rashi, *ibid.*, explained that Jacob never suspected Joseph of desiring to punish his brothers. Hence, enjoining Joseph from doing so would have been unnecessary.   (12) Judges 6:24.

Song of Songs, which is Solomon's. [13] G-d chose the people of Israel
from among seventy nations and called them Shulamith, as the Sages
commented: [14] *"Return, return, O Shulamith,* [15] a nation in the midst
of which the Perfect One of the universe dwells." G-d gave Israel the
Torah, which is entirely peace, as it is said, *Her ways are ways of
pleasantness, and all her paths are peace.* [1] All of the precepts of the
Torah bring peace to the body and soul. It brings peace to the body, as
it is said, *If thou wilt diligently hearken to the voice of the Eternal thy
G-d, and wilt do that which is right in His eyes, and wilt give ear to His
commandments, and keep all His statutes, I will put none of the
diseases upon thee,* etc., *for I am the Eternal thy Healer.* [16] It brings
peace to the soul because through the fulfillment of the commandments, the soul will return in a state of perfection and purity to its
source — as it is said, *The law of the Eternal is perfect, restoring the
soul,* [17] that is, to its original Divine source. This is the basis of the
Sages' comment: [18] "When the righteous leave this world, the ministering angels come forth to meet them, saying, *He entereth into peace.* [19]
On the other hand, when the wicked leave the world, angels of wrath
come out to meet them, saying, *There is no peace, saith the Eternal
concerning the wicked."* [20]

Great is the dimension of peace. Our Sages, therefore, sealed the
prayer [of the *Amidah*] with a blessing for peace: [21] "[Blessed art
Thou . . .] Who blessest Thy people Israel with peace." Thus, the
Sages said in Tractate Megillah: [22] The blessing of G-d is peace, as it is
said, *The Eternal will give strength unto His people; the Eternal will
bless His people with peace."* [23] Solomon likewise concluded the Song of
Songs with peace, saying, *Then was I in his eyes as one that found*

---

(13) Song of Songs 1:1. "[The Hebrew word] *lishlomoh* (generally translated, *which
is Solomon's*) is here understood as 'to the King Whose essence is peace' " (Shir
Hashirim Rabbah 1:12).   (14) Shir Hashirim Rabbah 7:1.   (15) Song of Songs
7:1.   (16) Exodus 15:26.   (17) Psalms 19:8.   (18) Kethuboth 104 a.   (19) Isaiah
57:2.   (20) *Ibid.,* 48:22.   (21) The *Amidah* is the prayer recited three times daily on
weekdays, four times on the Sabbath and festivals, and five times on the Day of Atonement.   (22) Megillah 18 a.   (23) Psalms 29:11.

peace.[24] Thus you learn that the preservation of the world depends upon peace.[25]

In Vayikra Rabbah, the Sages said:[26] "Chizkiyah said two things [about the greatness of peace]; Bar Kappara said three. Chizkiyah said, 'Great is peace, for concerning all other commandments, it is written, *If thou see,*[27] *If thou meet,*[28] *If a bird's nest chance to be before thee.*[29] That is to say, if the occasion occurs, you must fulfill the commandment. Here in the case of peace, however, it is written, *Seek peace, and pursue it;*[30] seek it in your place, and pursue it in other places as well. Peace is great indeed. Regarding all of the journeys in the wilderness, it is written, *And they journeyed, and they pitched.*[31] [The plural forms of the verbs in these verses intimate] that the people of Israel journeyed in dissension and pitched their camps in dissension. However, when they came to Mount Sinai, they were in complete unanimity, for it is written, *and Israel encamped there.*[32] [The Hebrew verb *vayichan* (and he—Israel—encamped) is in the singular form, which indicates unity.] G-d said, This is the moment that I will give them My Torah.' Bar Kappara said: 'Great is peace, for Scripture attributes certain words to a person in order to maintain peace between people. Thus, it is written that Sarah had said, *And my lord* [Abraham] *is old,*[33] yet when G-d related her words to Abraham, it is written [that she said], *And I am old.*[34] Peace is great indeed, for the prophets made such a change in order to make peace between Manoah [Samson's father] and his wife. It is written [that the angel said to Manoah's wife], *Behold now, thou art barren, and hast not borne,*[35]

---

(24) Song of Songs 8:10. (25) This is obvious from the fact that the concluding prayer in the *Amidah* asks for peace, thus suggesting that all previous requests depend upon fulfillment of this final prayer. (26) Vayikra Rabbah 9:9. (27) Exodus 23:5. (28) *Ibid.,* Verse 4. (29) Deuteronomy 22:6. (30) Psalms 34:15. Not only must you *seek peace,* but you are also to *pursue it,* meaning you are to persist in your endeavor until you achieve such goal. (31) Numbers 33:5. (32) Exodus 19:2. (33) Genesis 18:12. (34) *Ibid.,* Verse 13. A change was made in the words of Sarah so that Abraham would not be offended by her remark. This was done for the sake of maintaining peace. (35) Judges 13:3.

but to Manoah he said, *Of all that I said unto the woman let her
beware.* [36] That is to say, she needs only medicine [to restore her fertili-
ty, but she is really not barren]. Peace is great indeed. If the higher beings, among whom there is no jealousy, hatred, dissension, or
malevolence, require peace—as it says, *He maketh peace in His high
places* [4]—the lower creatures that are subject to all these evils—all the
more—require peace.' In the academy of Rabbi Yishmael, it was
taught: 'Great is peace, for the Divine Name, which is written in sanc-
tity, is erased into the water of bitterness [37] in order to make peace between a man and his wife [whom he suspected of adultery].' Rabbi
Shimon ben Chalafta said, 'Great is peace, for when G-d created the
world, He made peace between the higher and the lower worlds. Thus,
on the first day, G-d's creation applied to both worlds, as it says, *In the
beginning G-d created the heaven and the earth.* [38] On the second day,
He created things for the higher world, as it is written, *Let there be a
firmament in the midst of the waters.* [39] On the third day, He created
things for the lower world, as it says, *Let the waters be gathered
together.* [40] On the fourth day, He created things for the higher world,
as it says, *Let there be lights in the firmament.* [41] On the fifth day, He
created things for the lower world, as it says, *Let the waters swarm.* [42]
On the sixth day, when G-d was about to create man, He said, If I
make man for the higher world, the latter will have the advantage over
the lower world. If I make man for the lower world, it will have the advantage over the higher world. What did G-d do? He created man for
the higher and the lower worlds. [The soul of man is for the higher
world, and his body is for the lower world.] It is thus written, *Then the
Eternal G-d formed man of the dust of the ground, and breathed into
His nostrils the breath of life.'* "[43] Thus far in Midrash Vayikra. [26]

In Bamidmar Sinai Rabbah, the Sages said: [44] "Great is peace, for it
has been given to the humble ones, as it is said, *And the humble shall*

---

(36) *Ibid.*, Verse 13.   (37) See Numbers 5:23.   (38) Genesis 1:1.   (39) *Ibid.*,
Verse 6.   (40) *Ibid.*, Verse 9.   (41) *Ibid.*, Verse 14.   (42) *Ibid.*, Verse
20.   (43) *Ibid.*, 2:7.   (44) Bamidbar Rabbah 2:12.

inherit the land and delight themselves in the abundance of peace.[45]
Peace is great indeed, for it has been given to lovers of Torah, as it is
said, *Abundant peace have they that love Thy law.*[46] Great is peace,
for it has been given to students of Torah, as it is said, *And all thy
children shall be taught of the Eternal, and great shall be the peace of
thy children.*[47] Peace is great, for it has been given to those who
distribute charity, as it is said, *And the work of charity shall be
peace."*[48] Thus far in Bamidbar Sinai Rabbah.[44]

It is known that the peace within a city and the management thereof
is dependent upon the city leaders. The Sages commented:[49]
"Everything depends upon the leader. Moses was righteous and made
the multitude righteous. Jeroboam the son of Nebat[50] sinned and made
the multitude sin." When the leaders of a city do not conduct
themselves properly, dissension increases among their people, who
become like scattered sheep without a shepherd, as Jeremiah said, *For
the shepherds are become brutish and have not inquired of the Eternal; therefore they have not prospered, and all their flocks are scattered.*[51] *The shepherds* are Yehoyakim and Zedekiah, kings who were
unsuccessful in their administration of government because they did
not inquire of the Eternal as [the righteous] King Josiah did.[52]
Therefore, Israel was exiled because of the failure of its leaders.

In order to further the cause of peace, the Sages commanded that a
person should be sure to greet his fellow man, for greetings induce cor-
dial relations and increase love among men. A Sage[53] of the Talmud
praised himself by saying, "No man, even a non-Israelite, saluted me
first." The Sages have further said:[54] "If one who usually greets his
friend fails to do so one day, he is guilty of [the prophet's accusation],

(45) Psalms 37:11. (46) *Ibid.*, 119:165. (47) Isaiah 54:13. (48) *Ibid.*,
32:17. (49) Zohar, *Beshalach* 47 a. See p. 404, Note 72, in my Hebrew edition of
Kad Hakemach for the verbatim quotation. (50) See above, *Orchim* (Hospitality),
Note 40. (51) Jeremiah 10:21. (52) II Chronicles 34:26. (53) This was Rabban
Yochanan ben Zaccai (Berachoth 17 a). See above, *Matar* (Rain), Note
22. (54) Berachoth 6 b.

That which is stolen of 'he'ani' (the poor) is in your houses,'[55] i.e., "that which is stolen of *ha'aniyah* (answering) [the other person's greeting]."

Consider the great power of greeting, for our Rabbis permitted mentioning G-d's Name in salutations.[56] It is written of Boaz, *And he said unto the reapers, The Eternal be with you.*[57] Similarly, the angel said to Gideon, *The Eternal is with thee, thou mighty man of valor.*[58] All this is ethical instruction and good conduct commanded by the Torah in order to increase love and social relations among the people of Israel.

One should avoid dissension and people who are the enemies of peace, for it is known that whole kingdoms and communities have been destroyed because of controversy. We find in the case of the revolt of Korach, for example, that the punishment [of the rebels] included even *their wives, and their sons, and their little ones.*[59] The Sages commented:[60] "Four people are called wicked. First, there is the one who lifts his hand to smite his fellow man even though he does not actually strike him, for it is said, *And he* [Moses] *said to the wicked one, Why wilt thou smite thy fellow?*[61] It does not say, 'Why did you smite?' but *Why wilt thou smite?* Second, there is the one who borrows money and does not repay it, as it is said, *The wicked borroweth and payeth not.*[62] Third, there is the arrogant person, as it says, *A wicked man hardeneth his face.*[63] Finally, there is the quarrelsome person, as it is

(55) Isaiah 3:14.   (56) Berachoth 54 a.   (57) Ruth 2:4. Boaz thus used the Divine Name in greeting the workers in his field.   (58) Judges 6:12. This verse is mentioned to show that the custom of greeting a person with G-d's Name was used not just by Boaz but also by the angel when greeting Gideon.   (59) Numbers 16:27.   (60) Tanchuma, *Korach,* 8.   (61) Exodus 2:13.   (62) Psalms 37:21. This verse has been broadened to embrace the following thought: The growth and development of any individual is accomplished through "borrowing" the benefits and blessings of one's society. The righteous man, as the verse concludes, *dealeth graciously, and giveth back* manifoldly but the *wicked borroweth, and payeth not* back. The longer he lives the greater his unpaid debt becomes (Hirsch).   (63) Proverbs 21:29.

said, *Depart, I pray you, from the tents of these wicked men,* [who joined the revolt of Korach against Moses]."[64]

In Midrash Tanchuma, we find:[65] "In the future, when G-d will return the exiles to Jerusalem, He will do so with peace, as it is said, *Pray for the peace of Jerusalem.*[66] It is further stated, *Behold, I will extend peace to her like a river.*"[67] In Tractate Megillah,[21] it is written: "The blessing of G-d is peace, for it is written, *The Eternal will give strength unto His people; the Eternal will bless His people with peace.*"[22]

(64) See Numbers 16:26. (65) Tanchuma, *Tzav,* 7. (66) Psalms 122:6. (67) Isaiah 66:12.

שנאת חנם
Baseless Hatred

Love is either natural, like that of a parent for a child, or social, like that of two neighbors. On the basis of both of these types of love, the people of Israel have been called 'brothers and friends' / Israel, more than any other nation, should shun hatred, for our G-d is One / The sickness of hatred and the extent to which a person should shun this repulsive characteristic / The commandment to rebuke / The responsibility for the fault of the generation lies with the leaders who have the power of correction / The blessings which accompany chastisement.

Baseless Hatred

THOU SHALT NOT HATE THY BROTHER IN THY HEART;
THOU SHALT SURELY REBUKE THY NEIGHBOR, AND
NOT BEAR SIN BECAUSE OF HIM.[1]

This verse warns man against hating his fellow without cause instead of loving him. Now, love is either natural — like the love of brothers, that of a father for his child, or a man's love for his wife — or it may be social. For example, by virtue of the fact that two absolute strangers are together a whole day, there develops between them an identical feeling and determination in all matters.

On the basis of both of these types of love, the people of Israel have been called "brothers and friends." This expression teaches us that one should love his fellow man like a brother, and socially, he should be on good terms with him like a friend. It is thus written, *For the sakes of my brethren and companions, I will now say: Peace be within thee.*[2]

Israel, more than any nation should have love implanted among its people and should shun hatred, for our G-d, the G-d of the world, is One, as it is written, *Have we not all one Father? Hath not one G-d created us?*[3] We are one people, as it is said, *And who is like Thy people, like Israel, a nation one in the earth?*[4] We have *one law and one*

---

(1) Leviticus 19:17. "Because it is the way of those who hate a person to cover up their hatred in their hearts, therefore Scripture speaks of the usual events, but the law forbids all hating, even if expressed openly" (Ramban, Commentary on the Torah, *ibid.*, pp. 291-292). (2) Psalms 122:8. (3) Malachi 2:10. (4) II Samuel 7:23.

ordinance.[5] Therefore, it is proper that we, more than other nations, be united in heart and will.

Causeless hatred is a grave sickness, and it is the cause of all the sins mentioned in the Torah. It causes the hater to utter falsehoods about his colleague, and one who habitually utters falsehoods cannot receive the Divine Presence, as it is said, *He that speaketh falsehood shall not be established before Mine eyes.*[6] In turn, prevarification will lead the hater to concoct a false charge against his fellow and to testify falsely against him. Thus, Solomon said, *A false witness shall perish,*[7] and he further stated, *A false witness breatheth out lies.*[8] Due to hatred, one will feel depressed over his colleague's success and will rejoice over his failure.

One who develops this loathsome characteristic demonstrates that he is not a descendant of Abraham, for all of Abraham's offspring follow in his ways, as it is written, *For I have known him* [Abraham], *to the end that he may command his children and his household after him,* etc.[9]

Causeless hatred brings about a division of hearts and makes a person differ with his fellow without any regard for the latter's greater esteem. Instead, all wish to be leaders, and thus their opinions and hearts are divided. The Divine Presence does not dwell among a people with a divided heart, for the Sages commented:[10] *"And there was a King in Jeshurun, when the heads of the people were gathered,*[11] i.e., when they comprised one brotherhood." The prophet further said, *Their heart is divided, now shall they bear their guilt*[12] of the divided heart. On the other hand, unity of heart is beneficial not only in Divine worship, but even in idolatry. This is the purport of the statement, *Ephraim is joined to the idols, let him alone,*[13] meaning: "They deserve

(5) Numbers 15:16. (6) Psalms 101:7. (7) Proverbs 21:28. (8) *Ibid.,* 6:19. (9) Genesis 18:19. The verse continues: *that they may keep the way of the Eternal, to do righteousness and justice.* (10) Bamidbar Rabbah 15:14. (11) Deuteronomy 33:5. *Jeshurun* is another name for Israel. The verse is thus stating: when Israel's leader are gathered together in harmony G-d's sovereignty is acknowledged by all. (12) Hosea 10:2. (13) *Ibid.,* 4:17.

to be destroyed because of their idolatry, but since they comprise one band and share one opinion, I will be patient with them."

Unity is the essential cause of peace, and dissension and change are the roots of quarrel. Thus, on the first day of Creation, which alludes to G-d's Unity, you will find no discord, variance, or dissension. However, on the second day, when the initiation of change is marked by the division between *the waters which were under the firmament from the waters which were above the firmament,* [14] discord, contention, and change began. Accordingly, on that day, G-d did not say "that it was good," for the good was lacking because of the dissension. Such dissension manifested itself on the following days of Creation, too, and on the sixth day, Adam and Eve sinned and were driven from the Garden of Eden. Thus, you see that division of hearts, which is the characteristic of causeless hatred, stems from the second day of Creation, which does not contain the expression "that it was good."

It is known that the Second Temple was destroyed because of this sin. The Sages declared: [15] "Why was the First Temple destroyed? It was destroyed because of idolatry. [16] However, we know that during the era of the Second Temple there were pious people and men of good deeds. Why then was that Temple destroyed? It was destroyed due to causeless hatred." The Sages further said in Midrash Eichah: [17] "Moreover, [during the Second Temple era], the people rejoiced over the downfall of one another, as it is said, *When thou doest evil, then thou rejoicest.* [18] It is further stated, *And he that is glad at calamity shall not be unpunished.* "[19]

A person is obligated to shun this characteristic of hatred. There are many people who feign friendship for their colleagues while hiding hatred in their hearts. They make a pretense of being their friends so that they will not be on guard against them. Regarding this type of person, Solomon stated, *He that hateth disguiseth with his lips,* [20] and

(14) Genesis 1:7.   (15) Yoma 9 b.   (16) See above, *Eivel* (Mourning), Note 120.   (17) Eichah Rabbathi 1:21.   (18) Jeremiah 11:15.   (19) Proverbs 17:5.   (20) *Ibid.,* 26:24.

he further mentioned, *Burning lips and a wicked heart are like an earthen vessel overlaid with silver dross.*[21] Instead of saying "overlaid with silver," he specified, *overlaid with silver dross,* in order to indicate that just as there is no benefit derived from the dross, so is [there no benefit derived from] division of heart. Such a person deceives others by making them think that he is sincere, but his words are of no benefit even as silver dross is of no value. For example, Ishmael the son of Nethaniah [acted in this deceitful manner] towards Gedaliah the son of Achikam until he killed him.[22] Whoever habitually conducts himself in this way towards his fellow man will ultimately do so towards G-d, as it is written, *And they beguiled Him with their mouth, and lied unto Him with their tongue.*[23] The Sages wise in ethics[24] said, "One who has planted hatred reaps regret."

Because of the severity of this sin, Scripture has applied a negative commandment against it, *Thou shalt not hate thy brother in thy heart,*[1] for whenever there is causeless hatred and division of hearts among the people of Israel, the Divine Presence does not dwell among them. The Torah, moreover, was given to Israel only when the entire nation was of one heart, as it is said, *And there* [at Mount Sinai] *Israel encamped,*[25] i.e., in complete unanimity. Hence, *vayichan (and he encamped),* the singular form of the verb, is used in that verse. Similarly, Scripture states, *All the signs which I have wrought 'b'kirbo' (among him).*[26] It does not say "*b'kirbam* (among them)," but *b'kirbo (among*

---

(21) *Ibid.*, Verse 23. (22) After the destruction of the First Temple by the Babylonians, Gedaliah gathered the remnants of the people who had not been exiled to Babylon and attempted to reorganize life. However, Ishmael, a scion of the royal family (see Jeremiah 41:1) planned to kill Gedaliah because he considered him an usurper, and he came to him with cunning. Gedaliah was warned of Ishmael's true intention (see *ibid.*, 40:15), but he refused to believe it. Ishmael finally killed Gedaliah, and the people were scattered. Some, including the prophet Jeremiah, went down to Egypt. Thus, because of Ishmael's treachery which concealed the hatred in his heart, Gedaliah was lulled into a sense of security. Upon his death, the destruction of the national entity was completed. The tragedy of that day is still commemorated on the Fast of Gedaliah, which is observed on the third day of Tishri. (23) Psalms 78:36. (24) Evidently, Rabbeinu Bachya is referring to Rabbi Solomon ibn Gabirol, who, in his *Mivchar Ha'pninim* (Choice of Pearls), similarly stated this principle. (25) Exodus 19:2. (26) Numbers 14:11.

him), which means when Israel was of one heart. Had that not been the case, they would not have deserved the signs [which G-d performed for them].

Thou shalt surely rebuke thy neighbor.[1] This constitutes a positive commandment[27] to rebuke one's friend who is sinning. Scripture has stressed the verb "rebuke"—*hochei'ach tochiach (thou shalt surely rebuke)*—in order to teach us that it is not sufficient to rebuke someone only once. One must rebuke his friend again and again.[28] Similarly, the Sages commented:[28] *"Thou shalt surely bring them back,*[29] i.e., even a hundred times."* Similar thoughts are found wherever the Torah uses the double verb, such as: *Thou shalt surely open thy hand unto him;*[30] *Thou shalt surely furnish him;*[31] *Thou shalt surely lend him sufficient for his need.*[32]

Rebuke brings a person back to the Torah way of life. Thus it is written, *Reproofs of instruction are the way of life.*[33] Love of rebuke leads to fulfillment of the Torah, while the hatred thereof causes its nullification and leads one to the brink of denying the principle of faith, the result of which is banishment from this world and the World to Come. Solomon said, *There is a grievous instruction for him that forsaketh the way, but he that hateth reproof shall die.*[34] He is saying that one who temporarily *forsaketh the way* of the Torah will be punished with afflictions for his grievous sin. However, *he that hateth reproof* is in an even graver situation, for only death, not mere afflictions, will suffice for him.

The chief object in accepting rebuke is the rectification of one's character. If this is not achieved, the rebuke will have been in vain, for if one plows but never plants seeds, his plowing is futile. It is known that three things—plowing, planting, and watering—are necessary in farming. Similarly, the human soul requires three things: rebuke, acceptance of the rebuke, and correction of the character traits. For this

(27) The Commandments, Vol. I, pp. 219-220. (28) Baba Metzia 33 a. (29) Deuteronomy 22:1. (30) *Ibid.,* 15:8. You must help the needy again and again, until he is self-sustaining. (31) *Ibid.,* Verse 14. (32) *Ibid.,* Verse 8. (33) Proverb 6:23. (34) *Ibid.,* 15:10.

reason, Scripture compares rebuke to plowing, for in case of plowing the hard ground is crushed and restored, and in the case of rebuking, the heart becomes broken and contrite. Scripture compares the acceptance of rebuke to planting, for the main purpose of plowing is the seeding, and the chief motivation of the rebuker is that his words be accepted. Finally, Scripture likens the rectification of one's characteristics to watering, for the planting can succeed only with watering, and a person's acceptance of rebuke can succeed only if he corrects himself thereby.

In Tractate Arakhin, the Sages said:[35] "Whence do we know that when one observes some reproachful behavior on the part of his friend, he is obligated to rebuke him? We know it from Scripture, which states, *Thou shalt rebuke.*[1] If one rebuked his fellow but the latter did not accept it, whence do we know that one must rebuke him again? Scripture states, *Thou shalt surely rebuke.*[1] One might presume that rebuke is necessary even if it publicly[36] embarrasses the fellow. However Scripture states, . . . *and not bear sin because of him.*[1] From the verse, *Thou shalt surely rebuke*[1] we derive only that it is the duty of the master to rebuke his disciple. Whence do we know that it is likewise the duty of the disciple to rebuke his master? Scripture says, *Thou shalt surely rebuke,*[1] i.e., under all circumstances."

One who fails to protest against sin will be blamed for that sin, for it has been said:[37] "One who has the power to protest against reproachful matters in his household and does not do so, will be blamed [for the sins of everyone in the house. If he has the power to protest in his city and does not do so, he will be blamed] for the sins of the people in his city. [If his protest would be heeded] in the entire world and he remains silent, he will be blamed for the sins of the entire world. Rabbi Chanina said, 'What is the meaning of the verse, *The Eternal will enter into judgment with the elders of His people and the princes thereof?*[38]

---

(35) Arakhin 15 b.   (36) So in Rashi, *ibid.*, 16 a.   (37) Shabbath 54 b-55 a.   (38) Isaiah 3:14. The elders of the people are understood to be the leaders of the Sanhedrin, who as a rule are righteous people.

What fault is it of the elders of the Sanhedrin, if the princes have sinned? The elders are at fault only because they did not protest against the princes.' " Likewise, it states, *And I will cut off from thee the righteous and the wicked,*[39] for the righteous man will be punished for not having protested against the wicked. You also find that King Josiah [a most righteous monarch] was blamed for the sins of his generation, [and he was therefore killed in battle with Pharaoh-necoh, King of Egypt]. Scripture writes of Josiah, *And like unto him there was no king before him that turned to the Eternal with all his heart.*[40] Similarly Scripture states, *It is the sin-offering of the assembly,*[41] and the very next verse reads, *When a ruler sinneth.*[42] Scripture thus teaches you that the sin of the community is considered the sin of the ruler. Since he had the power to avert it [and did not do so], he is blamed for the sin of all. It is thus written, *And thou* [the prophet] *givest him no warning, nor speakest to warn the wicked from his wicked way, to save his life; the same wicked man shall die in his iniquity, but his blood will I require at thy hand.*[43] With reference to G-d, Job too said, *With Him is strength and sound wisdom; the deceived and the deceiver are His.*[44] He is saying that G-d, in His might, will punish the deceived and the deceiver, that is, the one who is led astray and the one who leads astray.

We were taught:[45] "Rabbi[46] says, Which is the correct course that a man should choose for himself? I must conclude that it is rebuke and the love thereof, for as long as there is reproof in the world, there is also gratification and blessing and evil is removed from the world,[47] for it is said, *And to those that reprove shall be delight, and a good blessing shall come upon them.*"[48]

----

(39) Ezekiel 21:8.   (40) II Kings 23:25.   (41) Leviticus 4:21.   (42) *Ibid.*, Verse 22.   (43) Ezekiel 3:18.   (44) Job 12:16.   (45) Tamid 28 a.   (46) See above, *Ahavah* (Love of G-d), Note 42.   (47) This answer should be compared to that found in Aboth 2:1: "That which one feels to be honorable to himself and which also brings him honor from mankind, etc." Apparently, since reproof is a matter of concern for society as a whole, the text before us is addressed to the community as well as to the individual. On the other hand, the answer in Aboth is addressed primarily to the individual.   (48) Proverbs 24:25.

לשון הרע
The Evil Tongue

The positive commandment of remembering what happened to Miriam when she spoke evil of Moses / The reason the Torah forbids us to join those idle people who gather for purposeless chatter / The great severity of the sin of slander and its punishment / Slander and shade of slander / The sin of slander is as severe as committing a sinful act / Slander of quarrelsome people / The great obligation to guard oneself in his speech, since the power of speech stems from the rational soul.

The Evil Tongue

REMEMBER WHAT THE ETERNAL THY G-D DID UNTO
MIRIAM, ON THE WAY YE CAME FORTH OUT OF EGYPT.[1]

This constitutes a positive commandment of the Torah[2] and is included among the *taryag*[3] commandments. It is similar in expression to the positive commandments, *Remember this day, in which ye came out of Egypt,*[4] and *Remember the Sabbath-day, to keep it holy.*[5] Moses our teacher thus warns us in the above verse[1] that slander is extremely loathsome and that those who engage in it are not worthy of receiving the Divine Presence [as explained further on].

With regard to this abhorrent practice, the verse is stating what happened to Miriam the prophetess because of slander. She spoke only

(1) Deuteronomy 24:9. Miriam compared Moses to other prophets. She also implied criticism of Moses' separation from marital life, something which other prophets did not do. For this mistaken slander, Miriam was stricken with leprosy. The verse here thus serves to remind us of the abhorrence which G-d has for slander, and that we should guard ourselves against it. See Numbers, Chapter 12. (2) This is in accord ance with the opinion of Ramban. See Commentary on the Torah, Deuteronomy, pp. 298-300, and "The Commandments," Vol. I, p. 264. (3) See above, *Emunah* (Faith in G-d) Note 32. (4) Exodus 13:3. This constitutes a positive commandment to remember daily the Exodus from Egypt (Rabbeinu Bachya, *ibid.,* — p. 100 in my edition). (5) *Ibid.,* 20:8. This commandment enjoins us "to recite certain words at the commencement and the end of the Sabbath, thereby mentioning the greatness and high dignity of the day and its distinction from the weekdays which have preceded and are to follow (Maimonides, "The Commandments," Vol. I, p. 181).

about her brother Moses whom she herself had raised.[6] She did not mention the matter to other people but only discussed it privately with her brother Aaron, and she did not repeat it in the presence of Moses who might have been ashamed and embarrassed by her talk. Nevertheless, she was punished with leprosy;[7] all her good deeds could not protect her from punishment. This is certainly an *a fortiori* lesson for other people. Miriam, Moses' elder sister, risked her life for his sake in the affair at the Nile.[6] Moreover, Moses did not mind her words. Furthermore, her words were not really slander; she only mistakenly compared Moses to other prophets.[7] If, notwithstanding all this, Miriam was still punished with leprosy for her sin, it is certainly logical that an extremely severe punishment will be incurred by people who really slander those superior in wisdom and age, and those who are sensitive to slanderous statements.

For this reason, the Torah has prohibited us from joining those idle people who gather for purposeless chatter. It is stated, *For a dream cometh through a multitude of business, and a fool's voice through a multitude of words.*[8] That is to say, just as most dreams are worthless and devoid of meaning, so are most of the words of a fool. By engaging in vain talk, one will eventually slander common people and ultimately even the righteous and the prophets. This will lead him to scorn their words, as it is said, *But they mocked the messengers of G-d.*[9] Finally, once he has become accustomed to disparaging people, he will then belittle Heaven by denying the fundamental principle of religion. It is thus written, *They have set their mouth against the heavens, and their tongue walketh through the earth,*[10] for their slander of mortals upon the earth has brought them to defy G-d Who is in heaven.

---

(6) Miriam, the eldest child in the family, helped her mother raise Moses. In fact, it was she who helped save the infant Moses from the Nile. See Exodus 2:7. Ramban, in his Commentary on the Torah, Deuteronomy, p. 299, expresses the same thought about Miriam's relationship to Moses, and he adds that it was upon Moses that "she bestowed her mercy and whom she loved as herself." (7) See Numbers 12:6-7. (8) Ecclesiastes 5:2. (9) II Chronicles 36:15. (10) Psalms 73:9.

Because of the severity of the sin of slander, those guilty thereof will not be permitted to receive the Divine Presence [in the World to Come]. The Sages commented,[11] "Four categories of people will not receive the Divine Presence: flatterers, liars, slanderers, and scorners." We find that David classified the slanderer among thieves and adulterers and said that the slanderer is not fit to study the Torah. Thus, he stated, *When thou sawest a thief, thou hadst company with him, and with adulterers was thy portion.*[12] He concluded, *Thou hast let loose thy mouth for evil, and thy tongue frameth deceit.*[13] Thus, he compared the slanderer to the thief and adulterer.

Solomon, too, spoke of the need to guard the tongue, saying, *A man's belly shall be filled with the fruit of his mouth.*[14] *Death and life are in the power of the tongue.*[15] In these two verses, Solomon thus informed us of the power of the tongue to achieve either good or evil. If one uses his speech in the study of Torah, instructing and causing the multitude to be righteous, *behold, His reward is with Him and His recompense before Him.*[16] However, if one uses his speech for gossip and slander, his punishment is ready and prepared for him. Hence, the beginning of the verse, *A man's belly shall be filled with the fruit of his mouth,*[14] addresses itself to the punishment meted out to the slanderer, and the end of that verse, *with the increase of his lips shall he be satisfied,*[14] speaks of the reward of the righteous man who causes the multitude to be righteous and who causes a community to do good through the power of his speech. The following verse, *Death and life are in the power of the tongue,*[15] is thus connected to the preceding one. It is stating that since death and life lie in the power of the tongue, one who loves to speak should ensure to limit himself to words of wisdom, instructions for moral living, truth, and peace. His reward

---

(11) Sotah 42 a. (12) Psalms 50:18. (13) *Ibid.,* Verse 19. (14) Proverbs 18:20. The way a person speaks, so will he be compensated. If he answers softly, it will turn away wrath, but if he answers harshly, it will stir up anger (Ralbag). In other words, speech is a powerful factor in a person's life, and one should use it responsibly. (15) *Ibid.,* Verse 21. (16) See Isaiah 40:10. In other words the reward of that person is assured by G-d.

will then be great, and the more he speaks, the greater his reward. The opposite is true of the slanderer.

We find this statement in the Midrash:[17] *"Death and life are in the power of the tongue.*[15] Everything is dependent upon the tongue. If a man has used his faculties in the study of Torah, he has merited life, for the Torah is a tree of life, as it is said, *She is a tree of life to them that lay hold upon her.*[18] The Torah is the remedy for slander, as it is said, *A healing tongue is a tree of life.*[19] However, if one has engaged in slander, he is liable to death, for slander is more grievous than murder. In case of murder, only the victim is killed, but one who slanders, kills simultaneously three people: himself [by incurring the punishment of death], the one who [listens to and] accepts the slander, and the slandered party. Is it more grievous to kill with a sword or with an arrow? To kill with a sword requires close proximity to the victim, but not so with the arrow. Therefore, the slanderer is likened to the arrow, as it is said, *Their tongue is a sharpened arrow, it speaketh deceit.*[20] It is similarly stated, *Even the sons of men, whose teeth are spears and arrows, and their tongue a sharp sword.*[21] To slander is to deny the fundamental principle of our religion, for it is stated, *Who have said, Our tongue we will make mighty, our lips are with us; who is lord over us?*[22] Slander is more grievous than bloodshed, immorality, and idolatry. In the case of bloodshed, it is written, *And Cain said unto the Eternal: Is my sin too great to be borne?*[23] Regarding immorality, it is written [that Joseph said to Potiphar's wife], *How then can I do this great wickedness?*[24] Regarding idolatry, it is written [that Moses said to G-d], *Oh, these people have sinned a great sin.*[25] However, it is written of slander, *May the Eternal cut off all flattering lips, the tongue that speaketh great words.*[26] It is therefore written, *Death and life are in the power of the tongue.*"[15]

---

(17) Tanchuma, *Metzora*, 2. (18) Proverbs 3:18. (19) *Ibid.*, 15:4. (20) Jeremiah 9:7. (21) Psalms 57:5. (22) *Ibid.*, 12:6. (23) Genesis 4:13. (24) *Ibid.*, 39:9. (25) Exodus 32:31. (26) Psalms 12:4. Scripture refers to each of the other three transgressions—bloodshed, immorality, and idolatry—as a *great* sin, which is in the singular. In case of slander, Scripture uses the plural *g'doloth*

In Midrash Tehillim, the Sages expounded:[27] *"I said: I will take heed in my ways, that I sin not with my tongue.*[28] Slander is more grievous than idolatry. When Israel sinned [on occasions] in the wilderness, the Heavenly decree of their punishment was not finalized until they sinned by speaking [evil against the Land of Israel], for it is said, *And the Eternal heard the voice of your words.*[29] It is further written, *Ye have wearied the Eternal with your words.*[30] It does not say 'with your deeds,' but *with your words.* Similarly, it states, *For Jerusalem is ruined, and Judah is fallen, because their tongue and their doings are against the Eternal.*[31] It is also written, *My heritage* [Israel] *is become unto Me as a lion in the forest; she has uttered her voice against Me, therefore have I hated her.*[32] Has G-d indeed hated Israel because of *her voice?* Has He not loved Israel's voice, as it is said, *Let Me hear thy voice?*[33] Rather, we must say that G-d both loved and hated Israel because of her voice. He loved her because of her voice, as it is said, *Let Me hear thy voice,*[33] And He hated her because of her voice, as it said, *She has uttered her voice against Me, therefore have I hated her.*[32] You must therefore admit that *death and life are in the power of the tongue.*"[15]

Certain types of speech constitute slander and others constitute a shade of slander. The Sages defined an expression of slander as follows:[34] "What is an instance of slander?[35] One who says, 'There is fire only in that house.' "[36] In Tractate Baba Bathra, the Sages commented,[37] "There are three sins mankind encounters daily and cannot

(great words), thus indicating that slander is equal to all those other sins which Scripture describes as *great*. (27) Midrash Tehillim 39. (28) Psalms 39:2. (29) Deuteronomy 1:34. (30) Malachi 2:17. (31) Isaiah 3:8. (32) Jeremiah 12:8. (33) Song of Songs 2:14. (34) Arakhin 15 b. (35) I.e., "what is an instance of a shade of slander?"—Slander itself is known. The question then must be understood as referring to a shade of slander. See also the following note. (36) Rashi *ibid.*, explains the implication of this statement: "In that house, which is occupied by a rich man, there is always a fire burning for the preparation of meals." This is an example of a shade of slander. See Rashbam, Baba Bathra, 165 a. (37) Baba Bathra 164 b.

avoid them: impure thoughts, lack of devotion in prayer, and slander. Do you really mean slander?[38] You must rather say, a shade of slander."

There are many people who think that the sin involving speech is not as grave as the commission of a sinful act. Therefore, King Solomon said, *As a maul, and a sword, and a sharp arrow, so is a man that beareth false witness against his neighbor.*[39] He is stating: "Do not suppose that the damage wrought by the tongue extends only to the sphere of speech and not to that of deed. On the contrary, it is as severe as if one takes a maul, sword, or sharp arrow, and smites someone with it. If you testify [falsely] that someone is liable to stripes, you have used your tongue as a maul; if you charge him by a crime punishable by death, your tongue acts like a sword; and if [you charge him with a crime punishable] by stoning, your tongue acts like a sharp arrow."

It is permissible to slander quarrelsome people, for it is said, *But me, even me thy servant, and Zadok the priest,* [etc., *hath he not called*].[40] One who fails to discredit people who are not conducting themselves properly is himself liable to punishment.

A person is obligated to beware sinning with his power of speech, for that faculty in man originates in his rational soul and distinguishes him from other living creatures. Therefore, one should take heed to save his soul by avoiding sinful speech. Thus, Solomon said, *Whoso guardeth his mouth and his tongue guardeth his soul from trouble.*[41]

---

(38) That is, why should you say that a person cannot escape slander daily? It is certainly possible to do so! (39) Proverbs 25:18. (40) I Kings 1:26. This was part of the prophet Nathan's report to King David of Adoniyahu's plans to assume the throne after David's death. Nathan had promised Bath-sheba, Solomon's mother, that after she would first inform the King of Adoniyahu's plans, Nathan would then appear before David *and confirm* her *words* (Verse 14). Based on the expression, *and confirm thy words,* the Yerushalmi, Peiah I, 1, derives the principle that it is permissible to discredit quarrelsome people. (41) Proverbs 21:23.

הלבנה

Shaming Someone

The sense of shame instilled in the Jewish personality entails discretion and humility. It obligates one not to shame or embarrass his fellow man by word or deed / The very purpose of the Revelation on Sinai was to invest Israel with the quality of discretion and shame / One should be wary of embarrassing his fellow men, for one who adheres to this sinful practice loses his share in the World to Come / Shaming someone is semi-murder / Shaming is a most serious offense. The wicked are imprecated by it, and the righteous are blessed by not having to suffer it / The applicability of the expression, 'It would have been better for man not to have been born at all, etc.'

Shaming Someone

THEREFORE THUS SAITH THE ETERNAL, WHO RE-
DEEMED ABRAHAM, CONCERNING THE HOUSE OF
JACOB: JACOB SHALL NOT NOW BE ASHAMED, NEITHER
SHALL HIS FACE GO PALE[1]

It is known that a veil of shame has been placed upon the face of
Israel, *the sacred seed,*[2] and it attests that they are the children of the
patriarchs Abraham, Isaac, and Jacob.[3] In the account of the Giving
of the Torah, Scripture has testified that G-d's Revelation [on Mount
Sinai] amid those mighty and fearful visions was intended to invest
Israel with the qualities of discretion and shame. This is expressed in
the verse, *And Moses said to the people: Fear not, for G-d is come to
prove you, and that His fear may be upon your faces that ye sin not.*[4]
Moses should have said, "that His fear may be in your hearts," but as
the Sages commented,[5] *"His fear may be upon your faces*[4] refers to
shame [about sinning]." The Sages clearly said,[6] "The shamefaced are
destined for the Garden of Eden."

(1) Isaiah 29:22. The patriarch Jacob will not be ashamed of his descendants any
longer, for [as the prophecy continues] they will all shun evil and sanctify the Holy One
of Jacob. (2) *Ibid.*, 6:13. (3) Yebamoth 79 a: "This nation [Israel] has three
characteristics: they are merciful, they are ashamed [to commit a transgression], and
they perform deeds of kindness." (4) Exodus 20:17. (5) Nedarim
20 a. (6) Aboth 5:25. The expression, "are destined" signifies that the road is open
for them to reach eternal bliss in the "Garden of Eden," and they will be assisted from
on high to reach their goal, but they must continue in that effort.

People will observe many commandments of the Torah out of shame, but when they are divested of that shame, they cast off the yoke of Torah and the fear [of G-d] from themselves and uphold injustice and pervert the truth. In fact, all the prophets admonished Israel concerning the loss of this sense of shame, as it is said, *Yea, they are not at all ashamed, neither know they how to blush.*[7]

Shame entails discretion and humility, as well as the aspects of scorn and disgrace. Discretion and humility require that one should be ashamed [to commit a transgression] before G-d and man, and the aspects of scorn and disgrace obligate one not to shame or embarrass his fellow man by word or by deed. One who is abashed before G-d will never shame others. Only sinfully wicked people who have no shame before G-d will shame others. We find the following in Midrash Tehillim:[8] "Rabbi Yehoshua the son of Levi said that Scripture imprecates the wicked only with shame. Moreover, it doubles the imprecation, as it says, *Let them be ashamed and abashed together.*[9] When it blesses the righteous, it doubles their blessing, as it is said, *Ye shall not be ashamed nor confounded forever and ever.*[10] It is further stated, *Fear not, for thou shalt not be ashamed, neither be thou confounded, for thou shalt not be put to shame.*"[11]

Since it has been explained that embarrassment and shame constitute *a grievous curse,*[12] a person should be wary of shaming his fellow man. If he persists in doing it, he loses his share in the World to Come. Thus, the Sages commented:[13] "A sage lectured before Rav Nachman, 'One who shames his fellow in public is considered as if he shed blood.' Rav Nachman said to him, 'Your statement is correct, for we see that when a man that is exposed to shame, his face loses its reddish complexion and becomes white.' Abaye asked Rav Dimi, 'What is strictly

---

(7) Jeremiah 8:12.   (8) Midrash Tehillim, end of Chapter 6.   (9) Psalms 35:26. The imprecation is repeated *ashamed and abashed.*   (10) Isaiah 45:17.   (11) *Ibid.*, 54:4.   (12) I Kings 2:6.   (13) Baba Metzia 58b-59a.

observed in the west [i.e., in the Land of Israel]?'[14] He answered, 'They
carefully avoid making anyone's face pale [by embarrassing him], for
Rabbi Chanina said that all of those who descent to Gehenna also as-
cend therefrom, but these three descend and never return: an
adulterer, one who calls his neighbor by a nickname, and one who
shames his fellow man in public. Although applying a nickname [to a
fellow man] is equivalent to shaming him, [Rabbi Chanina's intent is
that it is wrong to call someone by a nickname] even if he was accustomed to being so called. Mar Zutra the son of Tuvya — or according to some authorities, Rav Chama quoting Rabbi Shimon the Pious,
and still in the view of still others, Rabbi Yochanan quoting Rabbi
Shimon ben Yochai — said, It would be better for a person to throw
himself into a burning furnace than to shame his fellow man in public.
We derive this from Tamar, as it is written, *When she was brought
forth, she sent to her father-in-law, saying,* etc.' "[15] Similarly the Sages
expounded:[16] "[Before Joseph identified himself to his brothers, he
commanded his servants], *cause every man to go out from me.*[17] Rabbi
Shmuel the son of Nachmani said, 'Joseph greatly endangered himself
at that moment, for had his brothers killed him, no one would discern
the deed and no one would avenge him. Why then did he say, *Cause
every man to go out from me?*[17] He said, Better that I be killed rather
than expose them to public shame.' "

(14) The Talmud was written in Babylon, where the majority of Jewish communities
flourished during the third, fourth, and fifth centuries of the Common Era.
Simultaneously, however, Jewish community life also continued in the west, i.e., in the
Land of Israel, which was then under Roman rule.   (15) Genesis 38:25. See *ibid.*,
Verses 1-26, and Rashi there. Although condemned to death by burning for apparent
harlotry, Tamar refused to name Judah as the man from whom she had become preg-
nant. Instead, she sent him certain items which could identify him, saying to herself,
"If he confesses, well and good, but if not, I would rather die than disgrace him."
Recognizing the items as his own, Judah thereupon admitted Tamar's innocence,
declaring *She is more righteous than I (ibid.,* Verse 26).   (16) Tanchuma, *Vayigash,*
5.   (17) Genesis 45:1. Joseph ordered his servants to remove the Egyptians at the time
he identified himself, so as not to embarrass his brothers on account of what has
transpired between them. "But," asks the Midrash, "was not this a dangerous step on

We find that shaming is a semi-murder. The murderer spills the victim's blood outside his body, and although the one who publicly shames his neighbor does not actually spill his blood, he stirs it to leave his neighbor's body. Therefore, the Rabbis said,[13] "One who shames his fellow in public is considered as if he sheds blood, " but he is not actually a murderer. A philosopher said, "Shaming is a minor form of death."[18]

From the preceding, we can appreciate the gravity of shaming. In fact, when G-d wishes to imprecate the wicked, He does so by shaming them, and when He desires to bless the righteous, He blesses them [by ensuring] that they will not be ashamed or disgraced. The prophet Isaiah said, *Thus saith the Eternal . . . concerning the House of Jacob*, etc.[1] Isaiah assured his contemporaries that G-d would chastise them through Sennacherib, King of Assyria, until they return [to G-d] penitently and become worthy of being saved from Sennacherib's power. [The prophet continued], *And Jacob shall not now be ashamed*,[1] meaning that [when they repent] the patriarch Jacob will no longer be ashamed of them, for when children persist in their rebelliousness, their father is ashamed of their evil deeds.

The expression *Who redeemed Abraham*[1] refers to G-d, according to the simple meaning of Scripture. In the Midrash,[19] it states: *"Who redeemed Abraham.*[1] Come and see that fathers are saved for the sake of their children. Abraham was saved from the furnace of Nimrod[20] by the merit of his grandson Jacob. Thus it is written, *Thus saith the Eternal, Who redeemed Abraham, concerning the House of Jacob*, for He redeemed Abraham for the sake of Jacob." One may ask: Were Abraham's merits insufficient that he had to be redeemed for his grandson's sake rather than his own? Does this not indicate a lack of merit in Abraham? The apparent answer is that [salvation for Jacob's sake] would indeed have pointed to a lack of merit in Abraham if Jacob

Joseph's part?" (Tanchuma, *Vayigash* 5). (18) I have been unable to identify the source of this quotation. (19) Tanchuma, *Toldoth*, 4. (20) See Ramban, Commentary on the Torah, Genesis, pp. 156-160.

had not been his descendant. However, since Jacob was Abraham's grandson and a branch of his family, the merits of all Abraham's descendants are included in his merit and augment his distinction, for he was the founder of the family line. It is as if Scripture stated: "The merit of Jacob which Abraham contained redeemed him from the furnace. Since Abraham contained the merits of many [generations], he was worthy of salvation."

How grievous a sin shaming is! The Torah has warned us even when we must chastise our fellow man, we should not shame him at the same time, as it is said, *Thou shalt surely rebuke thy neighbor, and do not bear sin because of him.*[21] That is to say, chastise him in a way which will instruct him in the way of life, [but do not shame him]. Now, if the Torah instructed us to be cautious about shaming our fellow man when rebuking him for a good cause, it follows that for some unworthy purpose our sinful action would be heinous to be forgiven.

In *Ma'asei Torah,*[22] composed by Rabbeinu Hakadosh,[23] we find the following: "It would be better for a person not to have been born at all than to experience these seven things: the death of his children in his lifetime, economic dependence upon others, an unnatural death, forgetting his learning, suffering, slavery, and publicly shaming his fellow man."

The Sages' use of the term *halbanah,* [which literally means "making white"], is based upon the prophet's promise[1] that Jacob will not be ashamed, and that his face will not go pale [with embarassment], for his children will repent. G-d will then forgive them and show them His wonders, and the Name of G-d will be sanctified by them, as it is said, in the following verse, *When he* [Jacob] *seeth his children, the work of My hands that they sanctify My Name; Yea, they shall sanctify the Holy One of Jacob, and shall stand in awe of the G-d of Israel.*[24]

(21) Leviticus 19:17.   (22) *Ma'asei* (Deeds of) *Torah* deals with ordinary conduct according to the precepts of the Torah. See *Ma'asei Torah* under the letter *Mem* in *Rav P'alim* by Rabbi Abraham son of the Vilna Gaon.   (23) See Note 42 in *Ahavah* (Love).   (24) Isaiah 29:23.

אורחים
Hospitality

Hospitality springs from the virtue of compassion, which is one of the attributes of G-d / Our patriarch Abraham was the first to adopt and practice this beneficent deed / Whoever cultivates this virtue will merit life in the World to Come, and in this world he will be rewarded with children, as was Abraham / Whoever consistently practices hospitality is praiseworthy / Our Rabbis spoke at length about the great importance of hospitality / The prophet Isaiah urged us to practice this virtue which is highly valued by G-d, and assured us that whoever adheres to it will be amply recompensed in both this world and the World to Come.

Hospitality

AND HE [ABRAHAM] PLANTED AN "EISHEL" (AN INN) IN
BEER-SHEBA, AND CALLED THERE ON THE NAME OF
THE ETERNAL, THE EVERLASTING G-D.[1]

Hospitality is a mighty virtue. It stems from the characteristic of
compassion, which is one of the attributes of the Holy One, blessed be
He, Who feeds and sustains all of His creatures. Our patriarch
Abraham was the first to consistently practice [hospitality], as it is said,
For I have known him, that he will command his children, etc., *that
they will keep the way of the Eternal, to do 'tz'dakah' (charity,
righteousness) and justice.*[2] Abraham personified compassion, and so
we find in the Yerushalmi:[3] *"And he* [Abraham] *kept My charge.*[4]
What is meant by *My charge?* The Attribute of Compassion said,

(1) Genesis 21:33. The duty to love G-d, as explained in the preceding theme, leads
one to the love of man, which besides its many attributes of charity and kindliness expresses itself in welcoming wayfarers to one's home and offering them food and lodg-
ing. It was Abraham who first taught the world this virtue, and our author chose the
verse which first mentions it. (2) *Ibid.,* 18:19. As interpreted in the Midrash
(Bereshith Rabbah 49:4) Abraham would begin with charity and end with justice.
How so? After the wayfarer had dined, Abraham would bid him to thank G-d. If he
refused, he demanded to be paid in items that are unavailable in the desert, such as
meat and wine. Being unable to comply, the wayfarer would then declare, "Blessed is
the Eternal G-d of whose bounty we have eaten." Hence Scripture writes here first
tz'dakah (charity) and then justice. (3) This quotation is not found in our editions of
the Talmud Yerushalmi, but in Sefer Habahir, 191 (Margoliuth
edition). (4) Genesis 26:5. The verse is part of a passage in which G-d, speaking to
Isaac, refers to the virtues of his father, whose merits will be remembered by G-d and
ascribed to his descendants.

50

'While Abraham lived in this world, I did not have to do My work, for Abraham stood in My place and kept *My charge.*"

Our Rabbis of blessed memory taught that Abraham would go in search of wayfarers and bring them into his house. Thus, they said in the Midrash:[5] "Abraham's house had four entrances, one for each of the four directions of the world. Whoever entered one side left through a different side so that he would not suffer embarrassment of those passing on the road. Moreover, Abraham would go searching for the wayfarers and would run to meet them, as it is said, *and when he saw them, he ran to meet them.*[6] Scripture states of Abraham, *There is a man that spends, and yet grows richer.'*[7] For this reason, the verse, [*And he planted an 'eishel,'* etc.],[1] informs us that in Beer-sheba, where he lived, Abraham was heedful of this virtue and sustained wayfarers. The Rabbis of blessed memory interpreted[8] the word *eishel* as an acronym devised from three words: *achilah* (eating), *sh'thiyah* (drinking), and *l'vayah* (escorting). In Midrash Tehillim,[9] the Rabbis expounded: "*Who has roused one from the east, at whose steps righteousness was called forth?*[10] The nations of the world were sluggish in coming under the wings of the Divine Presence, but it was Abraham who roused them, as it says, *Who has roused one from the east.*" However, not only did [Abraham bestir the nations to recognize the existence of G-d], but he also awoke in them the need for charity, which lay dormant until Abraham erected an inn.

The word *eishel* literally denotes a tree, which explains why the Torah says, *and he planted an 'eishel.'* By interpreting the word *eishel* as an acronym [representing eating, drinking, and escorting, as above], the Rabbis intended to suggest that the mighty virtue of hospitality is analogous to a fruit-bearing tree, for by means of

(5) Midrash Tehillim, 110.   (6) Genesis 18:2.   (7) Proverbs 11:24. If one devotes his wealth to charitable causes, he will be bountifully rewarded for his magnanimity. The Midrash properly interprets the verse with reference to Abraham.   (8) Midrash Tehillim, 37:1. This interpretation is also found in Rabbeinu Bachya's commentary on Genesis 21:33.   (9) Midrash Tehillim, 110.   (10) Isaiah 41:2.

[hospitality], Abraham planted a tree for himself in heaven which would produce for him fruits [of reward]. Throughout the entire Torah, the expression *and he planted* occurs in only two instances: *and he planted an 'eishel,'*[1] *and the Eternal G-d planted a garden in Eden.*[11] This intimates that one who consistently practices this virtue will merit *Gan Eden*[12] [in the World to Come]. All of the commandments are like trees which produce various kinds of fruit. The trunk, however, which is the principal part of the tree endures. The commandments too produce fruits of reward in this world, but the principal reward remains reserved for the World to Come.

In my opinion, the verse, *He who keepeth the fig tree shall eat the fruit thereof, and he that waiteth on his master shall be honored,*[13] can be interpreted as follows: Besides his wages, the worker who guards the fig tree has the additional satisfaction of being able to eat its fruits. Similarly, *he that waiteth on his master shall be honored.* There are kings who surround themselves with guards not out of any fear for their personal safety, but out of respect for their royal status, and the guardsmen, besides earning their regular wages for protecting the monarch, enjoy the additional benefit of having other people respect and even fear them because of their close connection to the king. Therefore, Solomon devised this analogy of the commandments of the Torah [and the faithful watchmen], for when one observes the commandments, not only is his principal reward set aside for him in the World to Come, but he enjoys the fruits of [his reward] in this world. We thus learn that in this world, some of the commandments[14] of the

Torah entail varying fruits [of reward]. For [the observance of] some commandments, the reward is longevity, for others riches and honor, and for others children.

We find that the reward for hospitality is children, for this was the case with Abraham and similarly with the Shunamite woman, who offered hospitality to Elisha the prophet, as it is written, *Let us make, I pray thee, a little chamber on the roof, and let us set for him there a bed, and a table, and a chair, and a candlestick.*[15] She was a notable and wise woman, as it is written, *and there was a great woman,*[16] meaning [that she was] notable. Her words were uttered in wisdom and premeditation. [In the verse above] she first mentioned *a bed*, for a person who is weary from his travel wishes to lie down and rest more than [he wants] food. She spoke next of the table and chair and [mentioned that] at sundown, they would light the candlestick. [Thus, she arranged for Elisha's needs in the proper sequence of occurrences.] She said to her husband about Elisha, *this is a holy man of G-d that passeth by us 'tamid' (continually).*[17] "Rabbi Yosei the son of Rabbi Chanina commented in the name of Rabbi Eliezer ben Yaakov, 'He who receives a learned scholar as a guest in his home and invites him to partake of his wealth is [considered] as if he brought the *t'midim* (daily whole burnt-offerings) [upon the altar in the Sanctuary].' "[18] Because of this virtue, the Shunamite woman merited a son, who [later] became Habakkuk the prophet. There is an allusion to this in the Scriptural passage.[19]

---

between man and his fellow. The study of Torah, however, is equal to all of these (based on Peiah 1:1). (15) II Kings 4:10. The Shunamite woman said these words to her husband, suggesting that they offer the hospitality of their home to Elisha. (16) *Ibid.*, Verse 8. (17) *Ibid.*, Verse 9. (18) Berachoth 10b. (19) The allusion is explained in accordance with a text in the Zohar (*Beshalach* 44b-45a), which bases it upon the expression of the prophet when he promised her *thou shalt 'chobeketh' (embrace) a son* (II Kings 4:16). The word *chobeketh*—instead of *chabuk*—suggests the name of Habakkuk, one of the prophets, whose words are recorded in the Twelve Minor Prophets. See further on this point, in my Hebrew edition, pp. 37-38.

One who consistently practices this principle of hospitality and meticulously honors and serves his guests is worthy of praise and merits great reward. In Tractate Baba Metzia,[20] the Rabbis commented with regard to Abraham: "Whatever Abraham himself did for the ministering angels [who appeared in the guise of men], the Holy One Himself, blessed be He, did for his descendants, and whatever Abraham did for the angels through a messenger, G-d did for Abraham's seed through a messenger. Thus, it is written, *And Abraham ran unto the herd,*[21] and of the Holy One, blessed be He, it is said, *And He brought across quails from the sea.*[22] Of Abraham it is written, *And he took curd and milk,*[23] and of G-d it is stated, *Behold, I will cause to rain bread from heaven for you.*[24] Of Abraham it is written, *and he stood by them,*[23] and of G-d it is said, *Behold, I will stand there before thee upon the rock in Horeb.*[25] Of Abraham it is written, *and Abraham went with them to bring them on the way,*[26] and of G-d it is stated, *And the Eternal went before them by day,*[27] [the Eternal . . . Himself], not by means of a messenger. It is written that Abraham said, *Let now a little water be brought,*[28] and it is stated that G-d said to Moses, *and thou shalt smite the rock, and there shall come water out of it.*"[25]

Hospitality is indeed great. Our Rabbis commented about it at the end of Tractate Berachoth[29] as follows: "Rabbi Yosei began his speech in honor of hospitality and said, 'It is written, *Thou shalt not abhor an Edomite, for he is thy brother; thou shalt not abhor an Egyptian, because thou wast a stranger in his land.*[30] We deduce *a fortiori:* If the Egyptians were so greatly [rewarded, as the above verse indicates], although they received the Israelites only for their own benefit — as it is said, *And if thou* [Joseph] *knowest any able men among them, then*

(20) Baba Metzia 86b.   (21) Genesis 18:7.   (22) Numbers 11:31.   (23) Genesis 18:8.   (24) Exodus 16:4.   (25) *Ibid.,* 17:6.   (26) Genesis 18:16.   (27) Exodus 13:21.   (28) Genesis 18:4.   (29) Berachoth 63b. The occasion was an assembly of the Sages in the academy at Jabneh. While other Sages directed their opening words "in honor of the Torah," Rabbi Yosei and some scholars spoke first "in honor of hospitality."   (30) Deuteronomy 23:8.

make them rulers over my cattle[31] — then how much greater will the reward be for one who [selflessly] receives learned scholars in his home!' Rabbi Nechemyah began his speech in honor of hospitality and said, 'It is written, *And Saul said unto the Kenites: Go, depart, get you down from the Amalekites, lest I destroy you with them.*[32] If Jethro was so greatly [rewarded] although he received Moses only for his own benefit,[33] then how much greater will the reward be for one who [selflessly] receives a learned scholar in his home!' Rabbi Eleazar the son of Rabbi Yosei the Galilean began his speech in honor of hospitality and said, 'It is written, *And the Eternal blessed Obed-edom and all his house.*[34] If Obed-edom was so rewarded although he only swept and sprinkled [the dusty floors] before the Ark of G-d, then how much more will the reward be for one who receives a learned scholar in his home and supports him!' "

The Sages similarly commented in Chapter *Cheilek:*[35] "A little refreshment plays an essential role, for its refusal estranged two families [Ammon and Moab] from Israel, as it is said, *Because they met you not with bread and with water.*[36] Rabbi Yochanan said, 'A little of refreshment alienated relatives and brought near those who were distant.' It alienated relatives as in the case of Ammon and Moab.[37] It

(31) Genesis 47:6. (32) I Samuel 15:6. The Kenites were descendants of Jethro, who offered Moses hospitality when the latter fled from Pharaoh. Moses married Zipporah, one of Jethro's daughters. (33) In other words, Jethro's motive in showing hospitality to Moses was that the latter might marry one of his daughters. (34) II Samuel 6:11. Obed-edom provided hospitality for the Ark of G-d for three months. (35) The chapter in Tractate Sanhedrin begins, "All [of the people of] Israel have a portion in the World to Come." The passage quoted in the text here is on pp. 103b-104a. (36) Deuteronomy 23:5. Because of this lack of hospitality, Scripture prohibited an Ammonite or Moabite proselyte from marrying an Israelite woman. The prohibition does not extend to a female Ammonite or Moabite proselyte, such as Ruth the Moabitess who married Boaz, a member of the Sanhedrin, a forebear of David. Females were excluded from the ban because it was not the way of women to go out and meet the wandering tribes with bread and water. Hence, no blame can be attributed to them in this matter. (37) Ammon and Moab were related to Israel through their ancestor Lot, a nephew of Abraham. See preceding note.

brought near those who were distant as in the case of Jethro, for Rabbi
Yochanan said, 'In reward for Jethro's offer of hospitality to Moses,[38]
Jethro's descendants merited membership in [Israel's highest court,
which convened in] the Chamber of Hewn Stones [in the Holy
Temple].' Moreover, the practice of hospitality by the wicked averts
the punishment [due them for their sins] as in the case of Micah.[39] The
Sages said , 'Why did the Rabbis of the Mishnah not include Micah
among Jeroboam[40] and his companions who have no share in the
World to Come? It is because his bread was accessible to wayfarers.' "
[In Chapter *Cheilek*], the Sages further stated:[41] "When the smoke ris-
ing from the pyre [of the Tabernacle at Shiloh] mingled with the
smoke of the incense burned before the idol of Micah, the ministering
angels wanted to thrust Micah down. The Holy One, blessed be He,
said to them, 'Let him go, for his bread is accessible to wayfarers.' "
You can thus see the importance of a small quantity of refreshment,
for it averts the punishment due the wicked.

The prophet Isaiah exhorted us concerning this principle of
hospitality. He stated that it is highly valued by G-d, blessed be He,
and that one who consistently practices it inherits two worlds: this
world and the World to Come. It is said, *Is it not to deal thy bread to
the hungry, and that thou bring the poor that are cast out to thy
house? When thou seest the naked, that thou cover him, and that thou
hide not thyself from thine own flesh?*[42] He specifies *thy bread* [rather

(38) See Exodus 2:20.   (39) Micah dwelt in the hills of Ephraim. His house was
always open to wayfarers, a redeeming feature which saved him from punishment for
erecting an idolatrous image. See Judges Chapter 17.   (40) Jeroboam was the first
ruler of the Kingdom of Israel, which was established when most of the nation broke
their allegiance to the House of David. Jeroboam prohibited his subjects from making
the three annual pilgrimages to Jerusalem, which remained the capital of Judah and
the seat of the House of David. He also introduced idolatry into his kingdom. To his
eternal disgrace, he is known as "a sinner who also caused the multitude to
sin."   (41) Sanhedrin 103b.   (42) Isaiah 58:7. The prophet chastises those who
spend their day of fasting just perfunctorily and think that they have done their duty.
"But," asks he, "is this not the true function of the day, *to deal thy bread,*

than " of thy bread," which would indicate that you have an abundance thereof], to teach you that although you have but one piece of bread, you should share it with whoever asks you for it. *And that thou bring the poor that are cast out to thy house* . . . .[42] This teaches that if the poor do not come to your house, you are obligated to seek them and bring them into your home, for this is what Abraham did, as it is written, *and when he saw them, he ran to meet them.*[6] *When thou seest the naked, that thou cover him* . . . . [42] In other words, if among the poor you find one who is naked, you must clothe him, for you are bound to walk in the ways of G-d, blessed be He, as it is said, *and thou shalt walk in His ways.*[43] Just as He clothes the naked — as it is said, *And the Eternal G-d made for Adam and for his wife garments of skins, and clothed them*[44] — so should you clothe them. Job also mentioned this theme: *If I have seen any wanderer in want of clothing, or that the needy had no covering; If his loins have not blessed me, and if he were not warmed with the fleece of my sheep.*[45] . . . *And that thou hide not thyself from thine own flesh?*[42] This teaches that relatives take precedence over other poor. Our Rabbis interpreted it thus:[46] *"The poor with thee.*[47] [If you must choose between supporting] the poor of your city and the poor of another city, the poor of your own city have priority, for it says, *with thee,* meaning those who are physically near you as well as those who are related to you." The Rabbis further explained[48] that paternal relatives take precedence over maternal kin.

If you will observe these practices, *then shalt thou call, and the Eternal will answer.*[49] That is, He will answer immediately and will not avoid helping you just as you did not avoid helping your own kin. *And the Eternal will guide thee continually, and satisfy thy soul in*

---

etc.?" — This, incidentally, is the Reading from the Prophets on the Day of Atonement.   (43) Deuteronomy 28:9. See the text of *Emunah* (Faith) at Note 49 for full elaboration of this theme.   (44) Genesis 3:21.   (45) Job 31:19-20. In defending the righteousness of his life, Job pointed to his consideration for the needs of the poor.   (46) Baba Metzia 71a.   (47) Exodus 22:24.   (48) Sifre, *R'eih,* 116.   (49) Isaiah 58:9.

draught,[50] meaning that the Holy One, blessed be He, will fulfill and gratify your thirsty soul by satisfying it with the clear and splendid Higher Light[51] and will give you *free access among those that stand by*[52] who exist forever. *And He 'yachalitz' (will strengthen) thy bones.*[50] This refers to the tranquil rest of the bones in the grave. Our Rabbis commented:[53] "Rabbi Eliezer ben Yaakov said, 'This is the best of the blessings.' "[54] Another interpretation of the word *yachalitz* is that "He will deliver you from the punishment of Gehenna."[12] When one is saved from that punishment, he can rest and be invigorated, as one is refreshed in *Gan Eden.*[12] This is the meaning of the conclusion of the verse, *And thou shalt be like a watered garden, and like a spring of water, whose waters fail not.*[50]

---

(50) *Ibid.*, Verse 11.   (51) In the World to Come when body and soul will be reunited, the manner of how the body will sustain itself will be provided through this Higher Divine Light. This will be enhanced by the Glory of the Divine Presence and one's lofty perception of G-d (see Ramban, Writings and Discourses, Vol. II, pp. 531-534, for a full discussion of the subject).   (52) Zechariah 3:7. The phrase refers to the ministering angels.   (53) Yebamoth 102b.   (54) This is the best of all the preceding blessings mentioned by the prophet, for they concern conditions outside of the body while this blessing is directed to the inner health and well-being of the body itself (Maharsha *ibid.*).